The Ship's
Pasture

The Author

Well-known as a poet and from his poetry readings in the
U.K. and U.S.A., Jon Silkin is also the founder and co-
editor (with Lorna Tracy and Mike Blackburn) of *Stand
Magazine*, the quarterly of new writing. Apart from his
poetry, Jon Silkin has written *Out of Battle* (Oxford
Univeresity Press, 1972), a critical study of the First
World War poets, and *Gurney: a play in verse* (Iron Press,
1985), and is the editor of *The Penguin Book of First World
War Poetry* (Penguin, 1979) and *Wilfred Owen: The Poems*
(Penguin, 1985).

Also by Jon Silkin
and published by Routledge & Kegan Paul

The Psalms with their Spoils

Selected Poems

The Ship's Pasture

POEMS

Jon Silkin

Routledge & Kegan Paul

LONDON AND NEW YORK

First published in 1986 by
Routledge & Kegan Paul plc
11 New Fetter Lane, London EC4P 4EE

Published in the USA by
Routledge & Kegan Paul Inc.
in association with Methuen Inc.
29 West 35th Street, New York, NY 10001

Set in Baskerville 11/13pt.
by Columns of Reading
and printed in Great Britain
by Billing and Sons Ltd.
Worcester

Library of Congress Cataloging in Publication Data
Silkin, Jon.
   The ship's pasture.
   Includes index.
   I. Title.
PR6037.I5S5   1986   821'914   85-25638

British Library CIP Data also available

ISBN 0-7102-0841-3

Contents

Acknowledgments

I should like to thank those editors who first published
these poems. The sources are: *Agenda*, *Al Hamishar* (Israel),
Arab Times Supplement (Kuwait), *Between Comets: a festschrift
for Norman Nicholson at seventy*, edited by William Scammell,
Critical Quarterly, *Equivalencias* (Spain), *Graham House Review*
(US), *Hubbub* (US), *Iron Magazine*, *Ironwood* (US), *Jewish
Chronicle*, *London Review of Books*, *Louisville Review* (US),
Ma'ariv (Israel), *Menard Press*, *Minnesota Review* (US),
Moznayim (Israel), *New Statesman*, *New Poetry* (6), *Ninth
Decade*, *Not just another pile of bricks*, *Poems for Poetry 84*
(Poetry Society), *Poem of Thanksgiving* (edited by Paul
Kavanagh), *Poetry Australia*, *Poetry Ireland Review*, *Poetry
Review*, *Poetry Now* (BBC), *The Poet's Voice*, *Post Modern
Writing* (Australia), *Prairie Schooner* (US), *Prospice*, *Quarto*
(New University of Ulster), *The Reaper* (US), Schools'
Poetry Association, Sixth world congress of poets, *Stand
Magazine*, *Telescope* (US), *Thalatta*, *Times Literary Supplement*,
Wooster Review (US), *Words*.

Footsteps on the downcast path, part of which was written at
Mishkenot Sha'ananim, Jerusalem, 1980, was produced
on the BBC by Fraser Steel, and published in the US by
Michigan Quarterly and in the UK by Mammon Press.
The 'Salome' poems were published in the *Poetry Review*
when it was edited by Roger Garfitt.

   Autobiographical Stanzas were published by Taxus Press.

   The Ship's Pasture was published from Boston by The
Heron Press.

'The achievers' was given a prize at the Cheltenham Poetry Competition, 1985.

The achievers

Behind a front-door
stairs, without turn, or landing, run to a back-attic
in one flight; breath and breathing
go diagonally, as if
hand in hand
through the house, red stair-carpet and hall lamp
separating two walls that build
like stanchions
of light
into the roof.

This is Jesmond Zamyatin made
in his *Islanders* a Russian jest of –
shifting the tedium of yards, as he oversaw
the construction, and constitution, of Russian ships.
1916, the pole of the year: its ice.
A dithering of Ocean; the Czar's icebreakers
furrow dark water.

In a front-room
siding the stairs, a boy fingers
a flute, and a young woman, circumscribed
in a circle of light, shed from a lamp like a green bonnet,
stands a little
to the side, back a bit,
and bends above him to read the notes,
their closed dots and fins
silently filling the page

1

as stairs
fill the house, climbing
a magnitude
of soft despair
and achievement, coming on.

A paradigm

Here, mother, are a few words of love, meant
for Christmas and unfinished. But, mother,
I mean to give you love, a window in you in which
I see myself younger than I thought. Is this
love's face, I, who love, seeing none

but mine? Rather, a crooked tree,
its wood sawn from another, propped by
an engine's metal shaft, of the intricate
machinery of steam.

What use have I for the figure, its indice,
the closed dot on its open page? A *Kennedy's*
Latin Primer held shut in his hand,
the rosy cheeks recited a paradigm

the tongue cherished with ruthless Latin.

'A little naked son'

A little naked son at his father's shoulder,
with white belly and dangling member. He points
his father over the shingle – cog and mainspring
in grandpa's hunter. A town murmuring

in the cliffs – from on top of them,
a rope shaken its length, the eyes say,
with bees here, the flint, that look like bees
watchful over the vats for their multitude, rising
to amass honey, flickering continuous sheen
of labour. All the hive gets fed, she says.
Summer murmurs in her wings.

The boy faces the sea and won't enter.
His father puts in a foot; anguish at
sharpness of cold, at what he would
have his son perform, who waves his limbs
like a leaf, or aphid on a leaf. Christ,
his father mutters lifting a foot; he pours
a pailful of grey sea on him, and laughs
and asks if it is cold. It is cold.

A soft shrug of tears. Between leaves
and shade is a kind of concourse
where two can wander, unmoving. A hoard
of pale light off beige
mealy flowers – a linnet
his tincture of three notes she hears, her breast
faultless with his singing,
her feet squirming, the small vees – with wings
springing open. It lingers between them,

the birds that intertwined
with beaks, with energy, lifting away.

In the shade, the tree gives them as equals
as equal listeners to the flown birds
a temporary middle harmony
like a branch
of open blossom.

Taunton – Newcastle 1983–5

The government's comic

The ghost of a flea – Blake

If his mother bears
our child with
a torn brain, shall she die of it?
I'm the government's comic, my brief
to make people laugh. My existence
is a thread of spittle in their mouths. Here's
another version:

you are a droll beast, I its flea
an itch in the legislature,
my jaws out of proportion to my small eager body.
You shall be aware
of who I am

by my stipend. Where's the shaping life in me
to form my laughter in your body
in its long, spiritual laughter?
Where the blood in me, to help me feel
your laughter? I bite
you between the balls, the smell
excruciating. . .
the sweet flummery of blood
my child will have of me. On the day the sun

in its storm of making whole appears,
vivid and huge, to shuck
the shrunk, fitted iron
that bands the earth – and reveal
union and boundary, and raise
what isn't quick, until it is, I will make our child,
as they all are,
whole again. My Lord, my dear life, breathe

into me, until my limbs are astir
to lead him to a table, where the stamps – hinged
on sheets – I have saved for him
are no hobby – stare, stare away,
like the Minds of Nations, in profile, strong
as the gaze, the eye's
bearable magic. The bow!
God, bend your bow –
the underpinning of the eyes
the strong yielding bolt of the gaze –
and make the mind endure
all it has learned to fear.

Under a lamp

What was the dream, what? I searched
the mind's oceanic magma for congealed
recognizeable substance, muck,
for a spindle of meaning.
In the cerebrum, a phrase jammed
into its echo, 'Saint Pierre
et Miquelon.' A page
for colonials in an album,
a muted screech
of black children.
I tried to imagine hunger stepping
into their hunger
with my body.

A dream wash'd in sepia. I guard
a puritan in the civil wars,
blind vulnerable Milton whom
General Monck's victory would punish
with death. Milton? This man with me, his eyes
frightened, patient, is absolved of murder
in the peace. I bring him over a brown,
hardly lit passage, light
the colour of brown smoke. 'Sir,' I say
'by here', into a room where squire,
a blind star, offering light
but seeing none, enemy
to regicide, not unkindly sits
in the king's absence forming sentences
on a soiled bench. My arm
on his shoulders guides the prisoner
before our judge: one blinks at his hands
one stares at the other, mildness

and mildness. Light streams
up stairs behind him. 'Sir,' my arm
on thick stooping shoulders, for fear
of death. I said, or looked. Or if I said
or guided the man
before his judge on whose side
I supposed myself,
against death – this soldier
like a shadow under a lamp, is white.

What are these stamps? Saint Pierre
et Miquelon
I had thought
in the Pacific, tall people
with a black skin; these are islands
off Newfoundland, made cold
near the gulf of Saint Lawrence.
The head on the stamps
inclines, and drops slime from
its mouth, and then a gracious smile
of one who would kiss
those whom luck has vanquished.
Sir, I touch you before you die,
on the head, and press
you into an album. St Pierre et Miquelon
your finger-like children
clothed in hunger
and a polar fur,
their skin misted in the dark winter –
mahogany. A dream of care
inches across snow. The king of the poles
watches, with the head of a white eagle.

Autobiographical Stanzas

'Someone's narrative'

'no man ever treated of a subject that he knew and understood better than I do . . . in this I am the most learned man alive' – Montaigne

For a man's head

1

Leaving his eating-house refreshed, my father
carries the flimsy cash, most likely in
his inside pocket, buttoned to admit
his fingers. It is for a man's head
crayoned by fumes, a page of shapes
over the foundry wall.
And will the head come with me, and will it
concentrate a nation's charity?

The animalizers, benched in an eating-house
stare at the faces outside pressed to glass
whose grins are sickles. 'No,' my father says,
'that is not hatred.' Must I love these forms?

2

How shall I find my best way in the mind
this jittering world changes constantly?
The self is from its being taken out.

Acetylene: evacuated to a house in Wales, lit by gas

For gas, the house waters carbide, often meagre
for burning, though our lungs cough up a shred
of acid that we sicken on. Up at

plastered stone, flaky and gravid,
the sheep butt; smudged with an orange dye
wool inside mist wastes at the mothy house.
Then gas heaves. Quick, turn the spigots
across their limp flow, and ignite
this powdery whiteness damped to gas, a flame
that looms, raising a brightness edged
in a dark blister to a light shaped like
a woman. In this midst of war we see

a foliage of thorn, holly, as if truth
would have us pilgrims. Pollen off the grass
sprinkles, in dots, its future over us
as house, school, and jagged hospital
subside. The cracked dews prosper
in war's electric.

A sprig of berries, blunt and pupa-like,
oozes its juice on the ragged sweetness of
the ferns, although this crude mummering
lifts flame fretted round that first discourse
of gentleness, light. Our placid veins murmur.

Over the kitchen a bell widens its mouth
and closes it, each life between its lips.
We are to survive war. The bronze lights
its soft rigours on white, ribbed flanks
raked with scratches, as we lurch past –

small evacuated scars off thorns
pierce a filmy latent skin, as we scarper
beyond a hill. Death vanishes amongst
its stony quiet.

'We were evacuated in the war'

'sinking below the level of himself
to mark the insides of his head, like glass'

1

We were evacuated in the war
not working with language, a dull shrift
of possibilities, and sprinkled our piss-pans
with fool's gold. By us, two mines rusted
with real gold, quartz churches the Romans
split – septuagints that enriched in small
heavy handfuls. A queen's ring opened
a new mine, fifty feet under
unpumped glistening, a watery shaft
the eye retrieves. Invisibly air folds
round branches, delicate mainspring about
the sun, a sprocket that flicks up dew
at the flower's lip, misting dull gradual curves
of pasture. Like sweat, itching drops
barb this flesh. – I'd stop the Welshman inspecting
our fool's gold – Judah's pyrites – grained
by fanged sawing. If I crush and pan
valueless sediment, smelt fool's gold,
pawn it, and run off, I'd still saunter in
haphazard grass, bulbous blackberries,
swollen multi-eyed spit; even this house
dishevelled, I want; cursed, it is said,
to frizzle; on its flagstones blood speckles
in polish, where a master got knifed
balking a servant's marriage. For true gold,
authentic nature in dishevellment,
the hand abuses quartz to extract

fingers of gold, modest and noble,
splitting a Jew in Christian doubleness
of love for the community he serves.

Shy looks of England rust in the fool's gold.

2

So in dishevellment nature forms golds
neither as brutish as the other is.

3

I sniff gas –
carbide watered to light a dim house
where I am clean in a fee-paying school,
a pure scholarly, a large-kneed boy
whose brain squats, in it a carbuncle made of adamant;
not kind, bullied as bullying; a Jew
paying for to be educated in
the Welshman's English – an inauthentic metal,
whose herring-bone lines where a fat saw cuts
the lesser pyrites, at spoil-heaps.

I crush a childhood's Welsh indignities
of self-hood and inauthenticities.
Their fighting, brave: my crudity, a dishevelled
outsidedness, in large knees. Those boys
disarrayed merely, but yet authentic
in it with real gold, easy-natured
and brutal.

4

Oh, if the sun will arrive, top-hatted,
spangling each of us. Love lamps safety,
but I'd love genuinely, father or boy.

16

The woman's curve lunges at me, whose fruits
fasten my fingers to her.
I think this is the way the bush sings
at its growing.

Anxious with gifts

Anxious with gifts, they laboured between ruts
their ridges toppled, wavered over morsels
of quartz, the mudded drive parallel
with aching trout and salmon, trees diffused
between: came toward pond,
kitchen, gas-making shed, and turned right
to where I waited, clad dutifully in
the weave beaded with rain, that stung my thighs
like piss. 'Oh, come on', they said; I came
slowly, as if in sleep, to them. I kissed
my mother solemnly, father solemnly
and said, 'Come on, father: mother, come.'
Children with parents cram the house, as energy
swarms the creeper, a leafy electric
that we, here, have none of. Only gas,
diffusing a wet pressure, not burning,
of soft poison. Yet tables line
with heads of children, each a forbidden lamp
at play, supervised by teachers eager
to make their togged charges presentable
to parents. I said, 'My microscope-set, quick,
hold the slides, fine as insect-wings.'
She didn't. 'It's my birthday,' I cried, midget,
disconsolate, the tears powdery.
'That's enough,' they said, 'we're your parents
you've forgotten, re-making you in our
memory of you, and will even snap
your gradations of intelligence.'
Centred diaphanous gratitude, a web
to which I fixed.

The drive in ruts, with sifted ruinous

mud, wisped at the mosaics of
pebble – their hands huge and linked, mother
was radiant with pain. Ribbons fluttered
love in inducements, eager blandishments
of my dependence. Through the knobbed woods
the river specked with flux, a snake whose prim
triangle of raised head gushed clammy forms.

'Here is your knife,' he said. Second present,
with a silvery tongue. I drew its flash – and missed
the shrieking wood. 'You've lost it,' he decided.
My parents in interdependence, me – I hung
in whims of re-appraisal of sons,
feral, yet forced to return in need
meanly arraigned for its ingratitude.
But love is prodigal, poor, dependent since
the knife is lost. Its blade, shedding
drops of light, peters to nothing. So presented
to me like a toy, lost love re-formed,
its tears tied to each other on a string.

I come to you directly, out of love.

'The shrieking wood', but with a different sense, is a phrase out of
David Jones's *In Parenthesis*

19

Romano-British

'the war, the war'

1

Faces inside the wind's gusts smear us,
and heat lights in a bronchial mist; at twelve
I, like a pale face plied onto a stick,
a pole, from the hedge's swaying, witched
conical tufts of grass, but it cost me –
as if turned witless. I watched Rome's soldiers,
an infantry negotiating shafts
of rock, in patches of lethal shine; but not
much interested, I turned, suffused
with home, its rooms mottled with gas. So I
flittered over ridges, splayed tracks
linking my feet, rubbed up with diamonds,
platens of quartz, that joined and flowed upon
a courtyard, the cobble serried in
a jaundiced, diaphanous sun.

2

We ached with sleep. Waking in a faint
dot of screams, I rose up, passing
between upstairs walls, finding in them
a solitary room, its flowered rug
toggled with sweat. Over a narrow bed,
in white cuffed sheets, celluloid as dresses
a matron wears, I wrapped myself. Boys
rose in a line to be beaten, and, faced
from me, their buttocks drooled whiteness, on
thin attentive legs. The light, eating
furious dust, sprinkled a carbide light,

the carbide, that we damp to gas for lamps.
Violently a door slid. I lay
behind myself, in doting innocence.
And all the night would form in discords of –
not roads, or a silence on them, hung
in livid strips – was a train metalled between
Llanelli's columned slums.

3

The bricked riveted balcony at which
a door kept sliding clumsily – the supernatural
is rarely deft. Each boy had a red weal
bobbing its tiny jabs with blood. Spaces
of night throb, with artillery
aimed for planes. If I could tear my body
from this space, where my life thrums
vibrating military enthusiasms, I would,
as a man lifts weights not before
lifted, be strong.

Leaving

Like the beads of weft meagre
on their warp, war came apart, slowly,
with fatigued strength. I was fifteen. A dinghy's husk
lay awry in tidal light. Father
let me go.
As if I could.

And running to Victoria, its flaky theatres
of women, its fish-bars,
the salons of lost-property, here I unearthed
a cheap room. My tenant's mouth
creased in the landlord's eyes. 'I'll leave it'
I said, courage wetting
the granitic curbs.

The armed

'the actual duties . . . are not in themselves unpleasant, it is the brutal militaristic bullying meanness of the way they're served on us. You're always being threatened with "clink".'
– Pte I. Rosenberg, 1915

'what an impatient landscape' – a traveller

1

Like dew, spotting the hill's edge, lumpily
I left behind the town's lamps opening
like eyes, their insides; or rather, the insides of
a bird's crop, with its spurt of muscle that portions
a mash of stored half seed, half grit, onto
a sinewy gulf its effort concentrates.
I had this sense, leaving a place of coal.

2

Effort in winter. I was returning to
the camp, conscripted by the infantry
at eighteen. Coldness, pricking moisture
in slivers, I began a run, for camp
frightened me. Charge, sentence, and clink
at eighteen; odd conjunction of fear
with boredom made a threat, which the army
materializes, replica of exact
brutality, its mintage, boys. I turned
amongst light joined in shreds of continuous
blobs of light, which suddenly did not
exist, as if ingratitude had caused
its orange nubs to melt. The road curved to

my deviating straight tread; precipices –
all that was sheer, I felt, dropping onto
my knees to negotiate these imbedded
curves of blackness. Shame speckled my lips.

3

The instance became representative.

I came off leave, with a friend, reaching
the same village by nightfall; but this night
was hung up on the moon, a zinc nail
glowing curiously. Viridian forms
zig-zagged erect; oblongs of darkness
that the strip of road hung livid in had lakes
in shreds, gashed indifferently with
the land's edge. My friend, fearful soldier,
with long legs quickening from me, though I
begged him to wait, scissored his lucid shape
into the frozen valley, a form bobbing,
khaki beret, its badge lingering.

And I, judgmental without sense amongst
this plain light.

'Given a night's kip'

Given a night's kip, I had to climb
steps, to enter my bunk.
Bare women stacked by me, their pubis
and cunt like naked faces whose moisture
dripped off the page. Of what
use the women flat in journals,
my splayed fingers
fastened to their page? The phallus rubs
erect before an image.

Venus stands the other side of my mind
white, and shaking lightly. Her legs are stiff
and like her lips, apart. Her kiss
is enraged.

A hand

You came, a howl nearly. I said,
leaving for three months, 'you aren't crying.'
The bus piped, in starting, drops
thick and vaseline. For what does the phallus
quiver? the hand simulates
a fig, with my tenderness
in your image.

'At Hardknott Pass the startled road'

(for Gavin Ewart)

The startled road at Hardknott up among
the rocks fingers the contours. It is like
a waterfall. And jagged cyclamens
shake loose their forms, and pour them each side of
a milky cataract, pelted and itching
softness, wild cyclamens. You turned, lifting
your right thigh shaped like dropping moisture, that what
was made in you fruited itself among coils
of temporary life: wave-like and then
as calm as milk. So that the daughters live.

The mother draws her flesh up like a wave.

Absence and light

I shall get so used to absence I will be brought to more
    absence
than you from me.
It is a tree, a dim flossy absence
and a tongued florescence of wood. Take me, take me
in my absence,
you who know nothing of what it feels here,
you with your own absence –
apprentice stars
that saturate a dim chunk of space

and soften in flight like sodden fruit – fingers
with their touch in absence fallen;
stars out of blackness from their limbering masts;
but you, open
your mouth, speak, darkness of a sound
I cannot hear
you, silence, you awesome light that is loose and limb-like;

as if a tree, its opaque acid flesh,
its rings, perpetuated a radiance
in our two forms of one another's lingering.
A ring of acidic flesh biting in the soul.
And then the light, ashen and radiant;
this place of absentees renews itself
its space from which it grew, this radiance
in place of absence, if it is in place.

Given a Flower

'A field of grief' – Ella Pybus

1

In the violet fixes an acid leaf
through the smaller of two petals:
this life,
its exact strong
smirch of pain. You said, look,
these petals,
their mauve scuffed paper, a hue
getting pale. From your yard

each mauve flinching shape of light, you said,
mixes with the pale, the pallid
dark of a spring night. Look,
holding out your thin hands
the fingers bent, whose flowers,
whose the mauve, dense
fictions of twilight, streaked
with fingers,
the pale, livid nighttime?

2

An inseparable form
the mauve petal, its hem puckered – the mauve flesh.
No, you spoke, no. Furled
huntress; not as the bee goes for it, but virgin,
and like a priest,
you admonished love. The violet
shuts, in the verge in which it roots.
A whole earthen cavern of music

30

a vacuum of it. With dreams
of lovelessness
as the moon's shade peels off it.

A field of grief
in this snowy, glum light. You said, 'This is not
a future.' In this republic,
aching with snow, you walked
unsteadily away.

3

In this tarnished leaf printed in the overside
of the smaller of two petals,
matched and different,
the violet's life flickers. The flower
extinguishes like a lamp.
It is a penitential bloom,
the spring's want incessant
as the giving which famishes.

It is never nighttime. Its curd, that is a kind of dew,
is pain to the male sex:
I have nothing to do
with the acid sex of the violet.

Forms of grief
asperge the southern night, its salt sprigs
of blossom, dogwood,
the twisted star-shape, in whose hollows
salt curds.

Louisville – Newcastle, 1981–2

Winter bees

1

Winter bees, finding enough blossom,
of the sweet, small copiousness they cram
winter – frozen muddle – with amorous pressure;
the acetylene flare of bees, nectaring
in suffused purple light; the honey
cool moral, waylaid by feelers.

2

Flickering sugary flowers, their doused blameless
substance a gelid intermittent veining,
like strands of wintery heat – the bee hunts them
for liquor, jabbing a superfluity.
Veined blossom flickering, scalloped clouds,
        these consonant
sharing forms, a bee their suffering link,
is also a heated wire, quick form.

3

The zone forks its electrics, the sky, fanned
in ridges like a shell, splits with the flash;
the bivalve in a half form, coy fissure.

4

In cold this unceasing flare is work
a prisoner of honey slowly unwinds
as if it were a spidery filament;
oozed sugary superfluity

the jasmine hardly notices it yields.
The face is winter's

5

plum-coloured, a huntsman's hung up in the fog.
A doe, spotting soft grass and briar, her breath
gassed in exhaustion, inoperative limbs
tied as a thicket is, green liquid,
greasy manufacture you recognize
is gangrene. Recognize these shifting marshes,
the horse's buttocks, the man's slighter ones
a contour upon the animal fixed like
a grin, blood misting the thicket. Remus,
with fierce light, with struggling blood, as if
you ploughed up North America, tune your horn
with fierce light, with straggling blood – as if
the evening's silvery flanks, the gashed flanks,
the simple sun, gashed. Hot star, rise up, see
your furred contemporary, curious nectar
of the lonely; the dead wings, without weight;

6

the embrasures of honey, the queen's furred kinsmen
in rows and layers, effigies for the spider;
pointed receptacles, corbels of honey
fluted with dust, scum upon amber fluid.
The young boy shoves off for lunch, whistling –
his little pipes, the unbroken larynx, are reeds
of cheerfulness, earth for him so much down,
fluff, a mantle, on the bellowing cheeks.

The Wanderer

Fumes mist of gun-metal, with bits pricking
into a sunk light – I need
one to speak to in this murk,
my fiftieth year its archway, with fog

off the pole's lumbar region.
You fly folk,
I fasten on you a spidery form
quick as bindweed. And I can't

help it. A month back
the redcurrant's orb hung
two seeds, like a kid
supported in its womb. Rain

spots our linked hands – a sharp-witted
heraldry of love. Old stems
bear the redcurrant, new ones the black,
and memory is both. Half my life

I starved the womb, now I want
what she doesn't – who gives swaddling clothes
with a folded pram to the neighbour
swollen with redcurrant.

I've spent my memory. I'd rather
the staring wide-eyed world as bride.
The Thai funerary ship, rouged glass
on huge watery wheels, scores the street,

and smouldering flesh – the emperor's – his coat
is a black fuzz: the flies
are tickled to death.
I will admit, I prefer love.

Leaving *The Free Trade*

Ah, that's the heart of it; if we
could have free trade. A bar . . . yet what
bar is it? . . . one that
was a house. You stand close
to your lager, lightly warm. You smile.
Politeness is all the rage.

A tree that's grass, serrate leaves prick
off a stem – within the top
thick dots of deft, light
green pollen. The smells
of our class:
beer smoke and envy sift
between the strong lax fangs of leaves.

'Shall you leave early?' 'Please.' Wan smiling
in a white demeanour. Your heavy
animal grace. 'Do you prefer
this one?' – my grin stared at. 'What
is it?' as you turn
thirst to lager. As if a thing
in a painting, I'm
a trap, and rat smiling behind slats,
its head, that had
chewed its tucker, lowered
between the two scapulae, fur thinned
at where ears stiffen. We are
docile, becalmed. You: your moist
mindful, animal tenderness
is smiling.

35

This house, its ceiling
in lozenge tracery, a rose, is slicked
with murky pink, the bar
a furniture one must step
round. 'Love, throw the darts.' The board
chuckles within its rings, zinc
competitions – 'I will,' you
tell me – bull, zero,
thud of points entering rings. You put
your hand with mine. It's The Free Trade;

the eyed male minimum changes
to amenable companion, of a double nought
paired sequins, the two
nude bodies – us – heaving
that has scraped thin, paint
chipped off wood
in a pub with ship-builders
in a front room
of a seventy-year house built
to be modest –
humbling pain, the sweet
hot alteration, tenderness,
amour. I touch you. You are good
to me. 'You shall not,' you say, 'escape
as easily this time.'

The ships, all
shift from their moorings – in
a big swelling flight, fill with
departure, sail-ships
stirred with the wind – move down-hill
into the sea, through the arms
of their double pier. We are on the sea,
we are ships, from The Free Trade
the great chill amours of the north,

with lamps winking, gone.
The waves are furrowing themselves,
a sloshing aftermath.

Poems concerning Salome and Herod

Herodias was married to Herod Philip, and they produced a daughter named Salome. Subsequently Herodias divorced her husband and married his half-brother, Herod Antipas, but the marriage was condemned by John the Baptist on the grounds of incest. The story of Salome's dancing for Herod has become secular currency, but it is sometimes forgotten that Salome was no more than a damsel when she so pleased Herod that he promised her (mother) anything Salome should ask for. The price exacted by Salome, at her mother's instigation, was the head of John the Baptist.

See *Mark* 6: 17–29.

Salome's life

Look, she said then, made thin and small: I'm still
a damsel. Look, have a cigarette.
Ah, I say, no thanks. The mutant air weeps.

Go on, she tells me. 'I think I feel afraid.'
Well if you are, then, don't. The bed-shaped room
contains a primus and a fire. Chased limbs,

thin face, her buttocks fondled to thin moons.
– But kiss me, please. Or see here, a different prize.
She kneels, and, from a chest under her bed

she lifts the Baptist's head up to the light.
If you might wish this frizzled appetite,
I got it from my mother, beautiful

to any touch. And I will give you it.
She puts my timid fingers to her lips.
– It's in good nick. Saliva tissues at

the jaded casket, lips spout the preserve
of his mouth's wordy spiritual – death.
– So do you want it? but kiss me, I beg you.

To her thin fractured person the designs
of misery have touched her with, she pulls me
– but put yourself in, gently, and lie still.

She croons from her shrunk litany as much
as in her extreme youth she thought was fit
to serve and save herself.

Salome's Herod

His mouth jammed with 'incest', a lamp unfurls
its lurid flesh from darkness. That's so.
I steal strength from him, and in me
nurses his fragile time.

Now a'm a damsel, how old is a one?
ma foot havers, couldna keep still
th'thing; it clambers
and speeds, dappling
his eyes that are big
with th'Baptist's. Ma clothes flailing
a'm two powers to flicker
smiling
and ma feet, and to flex him
in my wavering blade-like movement.
I stop
and take off everything. To me
I take the Baptist's fluttered cry;
and into me
the King's products.

Salome's self

The rooted crystal lake
bleeds fish to the line; I'm tied to myself to flutter
like a damsel,
a breastless haired puberty. What
thing am I?

Limb and eyelid work, upon the tessellation
where ibex and fish preserve in the floor's pictures.
My hot self is pure space,
but his heated eyes dispose of me
in his darkness, whose energy silences him
in me. I am freed
upon another world, in which my silence
is a halo of ash at the wall grief
can't touch. Pity
and self-pity divide me up.

Where is the mother to abort or save
me? 'I will,' he says,
'be good to you.'
The disparaged soul dances, and dances
its disparagement. The opening
flower's parts were good enough.

Herod's life

Her self's innerness encrusts with
my liquid.

Breastless bare flesh, a painted smile;
and the haired mount
nests on the fork of thin limbs. The damsel bares her
contour of frail machinery.
Frail eyelash, her bleak future
in vials, a sort of perfume,
its stoppers irremoveable.

Maternal heat shimmies her. I
come on spidery male
legs, a little haired spasm pure
as an egg, to take my ounce
of delirium
with her's. The mother has her daughter
to do
the end of women.

In excruciated heat I run pure
of God's foundry, and cool in a falling
eyeless shape. To me
she's good.

Salome's John the Baptist

Where a cistern weeps lobed flowers
his absence and innocence
blur against a wall. The lily's tongue is full
of his truth.

The Baptist's flesh shakes away its caught lovely head;
I am the blood. Herod spangles with sweat.
My desire is rimmed by the Baptist's eye.

And 'no', he said. The body of every
man will be torn and reviled.

Herodias

e fango è il mondo – Leopardi

'The world is dirt,' a poet says. It's the wind
drops a crystal with a black root through water
to where toothed fish nose. The sink whirls up its mud.

My breasts are magma to children's wishes, and I
desire my provision. The Baptist spatters
Israel's veined lily, with a mouth of snow.

But I don't know who I weep for, or why. She
has work in dancing. Over the pictures in
the floor, performing on the tessellations of wheat
she bares herself. The soft immersions of
the Baptist inundate after all with his blood:
my forms of rooted water work free.

Three Poems about Grief and Fear

A socket of plain water

A socket of plain water. On my hand
the lake's obsidian congeals. I draw
a fish
a bearded wrinkle of fear. 'Immerse me.'

'Mercy is in the blood as much as blood
lingers in water. Torn from water, mercy
lies in your hand:

replace me in that sweet obsidian.'

Innocence barbs the lake

Hot hands: their fetid mercy sweats bread.
The palm hungers with its bribe.
The bread is a hook, and the baked meats
of slender grain lure our mouths;
this is the travesty of love
sodden with our element.

He stares at my face, mingled in his:
water, the eyes' strange pastoral.

Our bodies throng, touchy and phosphorescent,
like dew
at the flower's lip.
Innocence barbs the lake.

The sun's body, resting

Where light frisks in the shallows,
splintered flints in the water's radials.
A grin comes,
a flickering of darkness's mirth; the flower here
says it will live.

Bread is a burden on water. Here we thread
ourselves in fear to their watching: here
a flower is opening its waving spikes.
The flower is strong, it says that it will live.

As if soul were a glimmering aperture
the sun's huge body rests. Sacred with fear
we share each other's hinged timidities.
The flower is strong, the flower says it will live.

Envy of God

Fig, date, and balsam fringe
two pools, where shields rest
in Judah's desert . . . with gazelles hurtled
by fear, by fear checked.

Fig, gazelle, shield – words resting
by water, in desert where
that small king the asp grins. So we wait
by water to be at rest.

We are enough for Judah, and the shields
will suffice us. His psalms pluck
at our praise, that gleaming capacity
filling our jealous mouths with His name.

He made the wild places, I, too, form songs.

Climbing to Jerusalem

(for Moshe and Ziona Dor)

The locomotive, a short
satisfied fierce horse, scores the plain
after which five carriages jangle.
At the mountain's jointing, with anemones
that spot blood, glimmering orange fruits
like memory tumble. A stuttering olive
pierces the terrace with age, being adored
as if a woman of a hundred.

The denser patches of anemone blood
the higher we thread – you abandon us.
We strew energy as Jerusalem
helmets its stone; the herdsman, His shadow
fractured with sheep.
Pure absence measures
the plain we leave –

its celestial wounding – where the stream moils
between trees slender as astonishment,
their long flanks
dressed with fingers. Amongst
glimmering wheels of fuel
the sacred catches fire with the world.

Footsteps
on the downcast path

This poem is not concerned with heroes or martyrs, but
victims. And in that sense, it is intended as a history – not
so much the 'lachrymose . . . martyrology' of . . . the Jews,
which would, in any case, now be unfashionable, but a
selective history of them. This history runs from Roman
Jerusalem to the sewers of Warsaw. A Polish leader
recently remarked that the current troubles with Solidarity
in Poland were caused by its Jews. That there were at the
time something less than 2000 of them must therefore
attest to their ghostly presence, something the Jews would
not altogether discount. History is ghosts, troubled ghostly
presences. So that even if martyrology is not to the exact
taste of most Jews it is an ingredient produced by history,
and can only be ignored. It cannot be dismissed.

The poem is in the main concerned, historically, with
the Jews over the period of their dispersion, although it
finally rests in Israel as it is presently constituted. When
the Romans destroyed the Temple in Jerusalem in the
seventieth year of the Christian Era, they destroyed a view
of the Jews, or rather they assisted in a change in the view
of the Jews as it was held by society. Thereafter, society
saw the Jews, in their dispersion, as anything but the
people who had created the Bible. Cromwell's invitation
to the Jews to return to England was an invitation based
on their linguistic ability with Hebrew. The creation of the
State of Israel has once again obtained for the Jews a fresh
view of them.

The poem begins with the dismembering of the Temple, and moves through the expulsion of the Jews, from England in 1290, from France in 1394, their partial destruction at the hands of the Spanish Inquisition, and their exposure to hatred in Russia and Poland in the nineteenth and twentieth centuries. It rests in Israel.

What the poet must be careful not to do is trade on history, and to deprive such a history, as it uses it, of its factual truthfulness. There are many ways to distort such a history, and one way would be to use it as a justification for aggrandizing violence. Another would be to use it as the basis for claiming a superior moral stature, and as a demand for further studious suffering.

The protagonist of the poem is a Jew. He sees crucial Jewish events re-enacted over the walls of the Old City of Jerusalem, as he descends into it with his antagonist whom he has by chance encountered. This man tempts him along the lines of 'you may as well squeeze enjoyment from what you regard as the abuses of power, it's . . . they are – enjoyable. Isn't it, in any case, self-righteous to be a moral being? Aren't you likely to claim an unjustifiable, preferential treatment if you see yourself in this superior moral state?' The antagonist may raise some of the right questions, if for questionable reasons. In a mental sense, at least, this figure is bent on destroying the self-narrating existence of the protagonist. It is for the protagonist, this good liberal indignant Jew, to answer and not deflect these questions. Business as usual.

If history makes people, we, in our turn, try to re-fashion it. The poem is concerned with that attempt not to abuse this capacity, and with trying to survive it creatively.

I was not aware of anything mystical being intended in organizing the poem in six parts.

1

The tormented in a sullen privilege. Now
they are captors, and bind a naked man
to a wood horse. Then, they beat his soldiers
to his body, dappled with fear.
And for sustenance, in any case,
they tear him, beseeching forgiveness.

                    'Men at their torturing,'
a man said. 'These troubled soldiers, gulping
their leader – does it disturb you?'

                  The wood flinched,
as water flinches with wind; the aureole
is scratched off his chest.

                    'Anguish cleanses,'
he said, 'and it's anguish in these men, lapping
his blood. Come on, all it is is torture.'

A tree shakes with ice, fear shags me;
the fir innocent, his sharp grin sagging.

'Look,' he repeated, 'at this feast,
the eye innocent, the hand not.'

'I don't want to'

                    'but you should.
What a housewife you make. Doubting Thomas
passed into earth, and it got
a larger helping than he. These men
gasping, you can feel their pain, they feel it.
It's the way we are, each, contrite
for what's done.'

53

We get a move on, patrolling
this city of steps with a soldier's
muddy anguish. On each side
house-walls shop-walls
with moustaches,
sold calico, silk, the desert's spiky
rambling wool, and the stone walls
quickened on one side of us, or the other: chiefly the left,
on the left, always. Here is the first
stone visitation,
a tableau. 'Hear me, O Jerusalem,' I mutter. You,
heavy, petrol-fumed
like silk. We watch,
with sweat panic'd into the buttery stone,
a stone picture, the slab growing quick.
Women are hiked onto blocks, soldiers
hold open their thighs, as Roman flesh comes
in the woken belly.

                                           'Look,' he said,
'they are beautiful'

                            while, at their back,
the temple sputtered like upright matches,
the doric'd flames a burst tangle
of burning cries, the folded paupery
of bodies flammable
with soldierly hatred and rage, curtains of torn light.

'All joys are sexual,' he said, linking
his arm with mine.
                            'No,' I said, 'no.'

'Are you virgin, the coy sabbath resumed
in prayer? or something'

                            still pumping my arm
as if to spurt a ragged juice.
                                           'Yes.'

'And not attractive to you?'

                              'Each woman has . . .'

'All women are; never dishonour a cunt.'
And what else but squeezing the spirit
to tighten the candle's hot feather. 'Oh, my God,
what is preferable?

                              'This is torture'

'To not have is torture. To have nothing
is a mockery of creation.'

We walked more downward through the city, its
        crustacean
vaulting ragged. There was a second picture
in stone: three boats – each, a round prow,
a breast lifted.
Raised up to the sun, that between it
and sea, the English pennant shook its cross,
I mean blood. As if waves caressed
the wood's creaking sussurations, two mailed figures
lift children, with their frail
nuptial of parents, in gentle unction
to the sea's usury. England expels Jews.
The date crouches on its flag: 1290.

That first picture undid the temple, seventy years,
its squat fragile ghosts.
'History,' he mouthed, 'is wonderful, is its own pentecost
the brain of God exhales. Such suffering,
such parleying in stone, that batters
a skull someone's hands have carefully,
with consideration, put at ease.
Look, you speak as if your fruits were sugared.

Are you a decent man? kiss your arse then,
your lumpish testicles frumpish and sinning
as any.'

                        I turned away justified;
and as his purposeful destruction of me
sustained, we saw a third picture –

                               a stony hill;
in it a ledge, two men on thrones wearing
their gold, each head fitting a heavy crown,
with white hair, floss conferring sanctity.
In the soft mouths of Fair Philip, and Charles,
a torn shout – 'Juifs, Juifs – turn again, for you
pity is France.' So the ragged speech,
as trucks judder, when a locomotive startles.
A troop of families, at the alpine face,
half-exiled, alive in exile,
start downwards, like spiders clinging
textured crystal. The movement, hardly
set into opposition to itself,
than the mouths, 'Juifs, Juifs' –
stencilled a delicate 'no, go away.'
Families at the clambering seams. Two kings shout: 'Juifs,
this is the kingdom; go. No, do not go yet;
I mean go.' Open mouths at the dainty
air, the sun crashes onto a tor:
in cold desolations, splintered alps
speckle with figures. 1394, the date
freezes in air. Praise for my God
fills my mouth, frost, that spangles me.

2

In this hot country there is a dotted winter, hoar
baffling the mind of paraffin: a weak nucleus,
soft, hollowing forms of gas. The lamp fluxes a burning
    hand.

Virgins come, wisdom mingling with fools.
The big hand strews its quartzes of terse life,
hard structures with soft fuels. Careless and intense.

Spilt wax itches the curious hand Psyche searched with;
    foolish body,
her person charged with curiosity – that waxy
illiterate conjunction. 'There's no release
from foolishness.' That's what he said. I answered
'let's have something to drink,' 'yes' he said 'yes',
and we went.

3
Two separate events, two feet in two shoes . . .
the march, the slow protestant amble;
a pair of feet, many, like pelting rain – but the sound
in the lamp is like ash, its dots identical
and every dot comes out of the same flesh.
Bruised puce, bruised heart, the sea pulsing in it;
the salt is the same, as water is,
crossing its bed. To the bed it's the same – many stones
uprooted in watery flight. These ruined facts – ah –
as, ah, ah, to a stethescope's black cup.

A dais, with Torquemada, the face, plain,
its invariable smirk hot and boy-like. A tongue
pushes out lips pursed on mirth's quick. Quaint bi-sexual
    mouth
of lisped lippings, an orifice, a hollow jointure
of mouth on tongue. His candle the thick root
of his mind, a martyr's bed-light, singes so many.
Christ's proxy wets the hot earth,
staked into which not a cross, wood, – its projecting
metal length glansed, its tip a penis
on which men, the Jews, rest their genitals. Soot and
    melting,

57

the Vatican is ribbed vanes, a vacuous spirit
its night-piece, mucky fluttering angel. Weep,
like Ruth in the corn, having no home – weep
for Christ in innocence, for whom pain, they say,
and death were made. Jews sit on this metal jump,
corded by their necks to the upright –
a cross without arms – and their tongues protrude.
Look at the picture, if I seem to lie.

As the hands of the dark sisters death and night softly
        wash this soiled earth
the remnant searches a fresh portion of it,
as if who in this ambling soil could root. Who, and where.

4

This ragged city, a thalus on a pole,
blotches white the even-coloured psyche; at its foot
it buries in our soft dust.
'You are what I need,' the city spoke, like a girl
in the dormitory of a hostel.
The city spoken for by a single lamp, Jew or Arab.
'I need you,' she demanded, hair
wisped on the sun-burned skin, the blanket rucked
on the hostel's black-painted iron, a bed
braced with dreams. This city is a hospital,
sickness pitting its joints, with its split bags
of lavender. Its matrons are ill-advised
and ill-fed, but, in the market,
jaunty with spice and fruit.

Dreams in a ruck-sack. 'Oh, look,' he said.

'You again?'

58

        'Yes,' he admitted, 'this city's
soft-spoken ouzo, like an old client
whose eyes are milky with pain, won't disperse me.'

The stone devises another scene
as dust devises life, its shadow.
The lives of Jews dissolve in Russian, a lamp,
its flame lightly blue behind smoke. It bristles
with cherubim, a spume of exultation.
The Empress Caterina's bronze candle-sticks
spatter.
     'Wax is blood,' he said.
          Her Cossacks –
her riders' legs riffle, and bridle bells
flicker, softly jangled. 1881.
The Russian tongue is a strand in the officer's braid,
in his zinc badge – its artifice
a cock on a weather-vane the wind shakes through.

And then a stairway of familiar
more recent likenesses. Of Poland, its wars.

An archway links two terraces of homes.
May frosts its eglantine
that is not maytime, spring
dancing its thrush upon tawny grass.
Fire arrives, a horse brandishing flame – a mane
of thick steady arranged bands – catches
at shrieking wood and crevice. Girls
in a row, on fire. Hot sheen, blood
in ashes beside that. And wiring
that trails, then snaps – the blue cobbles slashed.
Armour's chain rickets on the flesh.
Sinewy cries, anfractuous crying; sweat, petals, shit,
and everything that one must do, to resist
in a Polish sewer. The House

up-ends its beard of flame, Warsaw, feathery
with soot; a fossil
gets smelted to a wall.

The working flesh of Polish gentlewomen
steps the downcast path. Spiny cats
trickle the streets, with lean inquiring faces.

5

For Jerusalem start the train with fifty lirot. Then,
springy, diligent as a goat, the locomotive circles the hill's
aureole – the buttery stone of which has a nub of fudge-
like decrudescence, viscous and sweet. We spiral – as if, by
reverse motion, we sank down; as though the down-spent
mind were, by stuttering connection, an urbs suckered
with flittering minds. Not so: sucked and dabbed at by
moths, we climb.
    Under Jerusalem is a sea. I purchase an unattractive
boat but the oars are made of Galil Cedar and give off a
wan dismissive smell. Lucifer abandons this cavernous
water, his fire dark; it is a cloak he has shed. No littoral
and no tide, but a number of crisp shells pallid for want of
light. I go to tie a hammock under the speckled orchards
of citrus – these fragrant cheerful lamps. This is a
mendicant corner of the Turkish empire, its moustache
fine as an arrowhead.
    At David Street, a man weighs heat, from fingers to
forearms a soft hot red, its greasy powder hairless as his
skin. This fear of death on him enflames a desire for more,
hot life. My friend smiled faintly when he heard this, as if
he were my diary.
    Returning once, we stopped to extinguish a fire that had
seized another bus. After, I was afflicted by the ragged
viridian of Cypresses that, notched with a grim demean-

our, step up-hill. If death tastes like this I may find it bearable. The pepper-man dispenses his red touchy ounces. My friend laughs on David Street. The talk of the evening sputters in Aramaic – Christ's year, with its wings of short stubby feathers. No more trees with the hinged mechanism of the cross, no more men springing fully armed into martyrdom: I want the cross to fold into a featureless stick. On the Temple's Jebusite threshing-floor I know that the wheat is about to explain, 'I am eaten, I am alive.'

6

A simple quantity of Hebrew spills.
'Is this a pogrom?'
                    'it is not' I say.

'Is all that finished with?'

                              The timbrel
in orthodox voices as they bind their shoulders
and pray. No, it is her hand dancing, her nails
that swish the light. If I'm alive, stone, not music
gives me my energy. I form a language
of chips and indentations in rock, scratches
and little pressings of momentary rest
the may-fly in her flight north left on it,
the bat of cherub wings, the family
pressure of angels disturbing the desert pebbles,
in their variety communal. I form words
and become stone. Praise for this to the designer
of letters.
              Dropping through this hell to a shaded field
I scrape another stone. The jerboa
fixes its little teeth into the side

of something smaller. Sparse cindery flowers
rub bees that like the insides of the plant,
the sweet wax food, spiky fractures
of blue and lightning, each feathery spike holding
a flame inside its own. I wait beside
these acid pauses, flower-like, my eyes
wide with surprise. I fondle surface, and its veins
smoky with tenderness spread, binding themselves
with bitter strength.

My friend smiles faintly, and his smiling is
a patch of bleeding on the tufted sand.

Drink, nightly, a small measure of dry wine.

Jerusalem 1980 – Newcastle 1982

Communal

(for Dennis Silk)

Prayers and rifles mingle
like legs of sleeping soldiers, like the mingling grains
in a stook. The weave sees
the competence of its collective life.

The cafe's a tattered flame, its fence
creosoted
in a distraught Mandate.
A Bible in one corner kneels,
its hassids
lust's tumbling Absoloms.
In reciprocal absence – both a space
and a grief –
some girl waits.
Breath from a great-coat speckles with the frost.

A man from the shipyards

In the process of becoming a Quaker, Penn, still in the navy,
asked whether or not, or for how long, he should continue to
wear his sword. 'Wear it for as long as thou canst,' Fox replied.
(A 'Quaker story' from *The Quakers* by A. Neave Brayshaw)

In the destructive element immerse   Conrad – *Lord Jim*

Penn, from the shipyards, bears a sword – 'natural
to a man of war' . . . 'what must I do with it?'
'wear it as thou canst,' Fox answers. Thou is
thou yet, although that natural, aching
psyche in its wet plasm of snowy
righteousness requires, 'your life for my child's'.
That some women
are not made more compassionate than all men.

As if for arbitration, with his sword
Penn leads the beasts – a forest clearing, by leaves
melted to twilight, the sword
like a bird biting
the leaves to line its children's nest; and not
much different, she, a human animal,
pulling his senses to her breasts, annuls
jealousy. Penn would change us,

the soul's light standing to its flesh,
its sleek shape, as charge;
he would merge the natural with the common flesh
as leaves with light merge,
where a community of stealth, of mild and fierce creatures
and dangling hair touching the breasts, gathers . . .

'not that we can't see,' Penn says, 'but the pain
because we do,' his sinewy mind
all-eyed, spotting like
a candle in snow. Penn and Fox

smudge with earth, lying between
friends, digesting the consequences
of hunger. They speak their minds, each day –
the leafy day, the branching night
in harmonious succession
– natural, again, most natural,
as when at length the living God
like living water
lifted his creatures up. Natural.

Penn took a fork from his pocket
as if he had meant to swallow meat. At which
the creatures shuddered in their forms, yet did
not creep away to weep. And tears,
which are the edge of grief, started, like blood,
the animals whining in upstart pain,
abandoned now, to be love's careless victims,
in that compact never to kill. Of love
they thought but little after that, as if
love, a watery human element – *in that
destructive element immerse* – were fit
for breaking, the lesser magnitude than care.
Then Fox's tears dropped,
the land held in his thinking
of rocks, sand, tears.

The Makers

He imagined that he should be transported to scenes of flowery
felicity, like those which one poet has reflected to another; and
had projected a perpetual round of innocent pleasures, of which
he suspected no interruption from pride, or ignorance, or
brutality – Johnson's *Life* of Savage

Lives of the Poets. He who wrote them listed
by, opaque as ink. Awry smile, as if
knowing the English Makers he ambled with.
A kind of honeyed community, worker bees
corbelled in their queer hive, who danced
in syntactical unison – he could feel
my eye on them. But though I hailed him,
the man who made compassionate sentences
held his smile wry and erect, and no syllable,
as if it were a farthing's worth of grease,
slipped past his lips. Discreet
as an emptied cup, or a churn made white
with used-up milk. I wondered, since

he would not speak – was it death
forbade communication, as Jews
have an interdiction against speech between
the living and the dead: no, it wasn't;
merely, he would not have an exchange
of touch or of words with, for instance,
– and in that instance lies the wretched fact –
those English men and women who have killed
the Irish, and sleep easily on it. Like wasps,
and not like bees, who sting and sting again
as if labour were not a jagged instrument
to be defended and broken, but poison's lance.

For whatever reason, not a peep
or smile could be got from Johnson. He left.
In the hive, the acid honey, a burr
of sound and work and feeding succulence,
lay in the vats, till our delicious innocence
should be more modest of itself, truer in sweet
atrocious delirium, and in
reluctance to be eaten, save as food.
Johnson had gone, I knew.

What we have held

> Here the patient stag
> Breeds for the rifle
>   – Eliot's 'Rannoch, by Glencoe'

This basket is a weave of rushes,
its sides steep as the rushy creek, with rushes,
a weave on an Indian
woman's thumb-nail, ninety years,
the brandishing wanderer's
nomadic plants; a funeral basket
containing those whom the English scuffed, their being,
        these squat fragile ghosts,
their temporary essence, scuffed,
like a rubber on a pencil mark,
but like a hand brushing water
speckled with light – the light stays.
And even so, they breed
as if for the rifle
of the voluptuous
revolutionaries. This woman's labour,
of which who is to speak,
is like an emboss; the impress
is hers, but the paper is that
of the people by the Skokomish
speaking Twana – a basket
with nothing in it, and fit
for everything. The woman's name
is *Louise Pulsifer*.

For Jessie and Sylvia Epstein

68

Crossing a river

Three barges, their decks of planking stabbed by nails
with gleaming oblong heads – their noise is moisture
from a horn, on offices, in which inky fingers
blotch the copies of claimants' letters. The river
they divide is a vein of filth, taking commerce,
with the sun dipped in it. I see pity crossing

the water. A town: pity stoops near it;
a cloud with sun in summer stoops with
a lumberman whose spine aches from his axe-blows
and the cutter's soft rasp. It aches, he says.
He and fatigue, two spoons in each other's shape
– work, workman, pity in one shape
of two spoons. I see the image and I see his shape.

Ajuga

In fine rain, a flower pricked
in tongues, off its stem.
Delicate virulent blue,
a bitter red-brown veining
the leaves, a hue Norwegians stain
their wood houses in. Blue, may-blue, sturdy
in all gaiety.
Ajuga: made of mercy,
never to pierce, in aimless torment,
its fellow.

It is to survive
from Europe in America, hid
in a small sealed box, its roots
such as they are, wrapped
in moist scraps of towelling. As I turn
from it, two roads
form a T of metal, welded
in blue acetylene light,
dismal dark roads, beside which sandy earth
hugs dry lumps of quartz,
the T rubbered in a skin off hot tyres – the mid-west's
colourless summer: bleak sun
on pale earth,
the mottled festoons of withering.
A man's torn mind holds
in his porch-seat swinging from
thin chain.

But here, thin pipe roots
of blue dark flowers
glowing like labradorite vessels used

as ballast – ballast-flowers,
like medals, like hearts, like a cat's tongue
poking. You advance
in delicate strength, in joyful
meekness; in me, like ducts, the swift
inturned evasions feeding
the soul's vena cava. Root your ghost
in me, annul violence
here, none knows why.
In this frosted garden, this icy suburb,
in great bleak notes, triumphants
of winter – hot blue flower –
Ajuga – comedian, voiceless
in the garden's clenched hand.

There is a wood, shingle house picked
in scales, a cobalt evening
a dry dark seethe
in milky sands, and a thread
of gannet's flight
with feet extended: the blue flower
as intense here.

This chronic disposition
these sounds of life together.

Four poems from the Chinese

The garden grows darker

Energy clarifies in the twilight
in dusk's shade clouds straggle and settle;
the curtain of twilight with a light breeze freshens
scraps of light glimmer the green and blue wood.
In the window, this light goes out.
The garden is touched with desolation,
its green pool flutters white, the white of plain fluttering
    silk . . . birds.

A cold noise is the feeling of autumn.
If one loves, the beloved shares an identical love;
strings of an instrument become concordant: wine gives a
    transit,
a journey, dispersion.

Unused to

Autumn wind is crystal
and white dew turns to morning frost;
at sunset branches are pliant, by dawn have stiffened,
yellow leaves that had in the day a green life.
From clouds emerges a bright moon . . . as from a cliff
and causes a pure flow of white light, a flow of plain silk.

The balcony can watch a forecourt,
'ao-ao', the hungry cries of geese during the day: up they
whirl.

A clear refined vision over four seas, the empire's territory;
the lonely disemployed one meanders within an empty
hall.

The heights of Wu mountain

Imagine Mount Wu, which a woman – the shaman –
possesses,
and a thin mist over a crooked terrace that faces into the
bright south;
coloured mist rolls up, rolls off,
monkeys and birds stop their speech, and start up again
. . . such beauty – as if it could be anticipated.

Waking confused words, confused within your gaze.
We sit in each other's mutual longing;
a green courtyard discolours with an autumn wind.

The passes

Mist bulks the space between mountains
from amid bamboo, the sun falls;
birds lift into the spaces under eaves . . . the wind is free
of the cloud-forms the pass holds.

Crossing to Europe

'As hovering – seen – through fog –'
                    – Emily Dickinson, 'A solemn thing' (271)

Light with frost burned, a natural doubleness
to which the mind shapes itself . . . and drifts . . .
the frail boat, insect, of mast and cross-parts
with haired rigging. In the cabin, three
hands, doggo. The bare mind makes
what it can of itself – the prow in
unequal exchanges with water pierces
never tears eternity. Work

is the ship's covenant, with oil.
I lie in my cabin, astute, under lamps
whose brassy discs of light soften at my cheek.
It's what work becomes, melted in love
to ease, though the double human creature
produces pangs of birth that men escape.
In the nature of water I'm absorbed.

I know I'm salt, thinking oblivion;
this swill is my life's transforming, and I,
full savour of it. Flaky with it
I begin to harden, through and through I'm salt
in a middling petrifaction; but to what

I see preferable, Europe, a tassel
of greasy lights – its congregation of
flesh making ash, enough to stuff a house,
though in burning they say we renew: and still
the wispy soul reposes in another's death,
so that as the ship hovers mid-channel
it chuckles, as if its keel rasped pebble,

as if the channel's shallows rip, is it, the thin
limb-like underlife of our craft.

Almighty God, I mumble, mercy on him
mercy – who carved the creature from its shade
the whale's torn shadow, from the whale – mercy
for the spotted larceny of flies
and for the tingling mollusc – its wet beige

Naming souls

An hour is held deep, in the underneath of time.
In the religion of purification
men's innerness
stands stripped of garments in the dusk
and prays to see God's image. Ah, if only I could bear up
the cup of bitterness,
my eyes turned inwards, I would drink to the terror in
    the eyes
of soldiers, brothers whom I fought with
and reached the Sawa's water.

They fell, tangled on the wire,
their feet raised high,
and that wail, essence of their dying, lasted only
a moment; they died, then,
very dark.

I stood on my own, the last
of the species that fight,
seeing these brothers, with feet turned upwards, growing
until they reached the sky, in death,
to kick it. I saw
the moon like an animal
rub a silver face on the worn nails in the boots
of upturned soldiers.

This fearful glowing on the nails in the boots of the dead
who kick at God, electrified
my being with a terror
that shone as if I were dying. With the flesh's
eyes, I saw the divine
in fear's mystery, in men falling. I cried

then, as if I were the last to cry
who never again in life
will cry what I wept
on the Sawa's water.

Translated from the Hebrew of Uri Zvi Greenberg by Ezra
Spicehandler and the author.

Before Mundheim

A man comes toward me, his sledge-hammer,
like a toe, slung at his shoulder. Serving
time. In Norway, servitude
is freedom bound in usefulness. He sways
with the pale blob of his hammer that presses
his gristly shoulder, and collar-bone,
on which the haft, shining with use
and sweat, rests. I fear him.

That is nothing. Promise of esteem is nothing
to him. The stone is his, length
of time, length of haft and line
of cleavage in grey green boulders
strewn by what is fugitive in
a fighter, the huge chunks
of explosion. If my father dies, he says,
I shall forgive no one. In a lake

not deep or sufficient for the salt
dimensions of a fjord, there stains
fir-clad hill, with large
thorns of conifer – mottled savageries
beauty in deep water turns to,
God's bristling things, this image
clear as the thought that rubs until
the factual roughnesses go;
no death for the image beauty turns
to in deep water. The reflection

sees hill, trees, grasses like hair
climbing against the sorrel,
milkmaid's knee, if it
exists, cow-parsley – the man

with hammer walks through me into
the foundations of the lake, punishment and crime
drowning, in Norwegian water that holds

what it sees – a village eking out
its mild nature, white and spiky church,
three houses, with loading lofts without
pulley and block, the stream
gliding onto the lake. I cling to him
in his drowning, in fir-like water,
my crime as nothing in his death.

From GURNEY: Gurney's poem

How to make a jib that lifts the maiden fern.
If a spray of leaf,
tooth, or hair, abandons itself
to the claws that should be hands, –
intent on handling – it will crush.
The leaves crush foolishly and spray in handling.

How take nature in modern hands, how give
the dockland man, his hefty male child
and cheeky painted daughter, the bent contour of earth, –
a pink campion
stepping on black soil. The barge

sifts through pasture, its working man
smudges his fag in oil and clay, this tandem
of dirt.

The lamps of home

Do my ears burning, does my face, mean
you remember pulling-to the door
of a flat, so close to the lines the traction
of locomotive and freight went
through us, our moist coy sex minted
with another's? As if you
were a house entered, a soft rage
of three in two pairs, of stars,
spearheads in a scuffle
of metal. 'Absence,' I exclaim

like metal scraped on itself.
The word lights up a terrace house,
or barn, that houses warm cattle
with their baled grass. Some small regular
gift is made, a sandwich cut
and wrapped for a wife leaving on her night-shift.
She nurses
the morose septic hours.

A car travels a coast-road. Flimsy light
from its lamps mixes
the driver's life in misty strands
with this absence of light. He sings, a high
cracked tin sound. The border
brings to his homecoming
two daughters and a son,
whose lamps disperse distance.
A son with red cheeks, their hue
in the blood.

His lamps turn the mist; but on
the moon's cracks tides fill
in, as if death approached. They swish
in denial; not so soon, they say,
his energy is theirs. The ruff
of the moon in tides swelling
across her face
in icy boisterous movements.

Newcastle 1982–5

The ship's pasture

In the sun, the leaf, hesitant but active
this florescence of plain wood; with joy
I saw the fields of England, as new, chartered
shapes, bargained for, and so, snipped
with standing sheep, their snowy garments
by the limestone walls, bulbous fossils,
their thick inert forms braids dangling
the soft wealth of England: Selah. Except
some people here are brutal, the fist,
because of standing in the wrong place,
at the cheekbone. Fist, or snide
arrowy word.

I rose from England much refreshed, but returned
at evening; much undone that was once good
prior to this mean juncture. It was joy,
beside my self, to see the new fields. Whose
is this land that, like waiting flesh, turns
with a kiss, domestic, but yet is
a local habitation with no substance or name
sustaining it? It is the ship's pasture,
its interlinking husk of submarine,
sea-spike, the sleeted fields of destruction:
for payment, for emolument. I am
a part of this – the bee, cutter of wood,
whose timbered house is unimaginably
hospitable. This is what it is. Northwards,
a new Jerusalem with the lamb lies separate,
its shade dense and lovely. The woman
starts again, as though each portion of this
were knit afresh.

We stock the deer-park

We are the deer-park, this truth is
self-evident? So that war, your
next one . . . in the plane, you,
a long-legged rodent,
are angled in the seat, limbs trailing
large brogue shoes that splay
frog's feet. You grip
a manual of war,
the finger nails wanting blood
their moons a misty lunar white.

The rat's bubonic
swelling under the eyes opens,
with odourless sticky threads, the matter
of new wars. 'Yes, sir',
his whiskerless face at ease
with obedience. And soon
the results of our obediences,
the groin's swollen stuffs, the armpit's broken
lump, arm that can't ease
against its well-shaped flank, and chest, the whole trunk
in its disposition of gaiety.
I have seen
the sharp, physical
shreds of London,
after incendiaries. War,
its intimate plague, creeping about
like the rat's whiskered
twitching sniff at us,
our intimate parts exposed.

Ah, sir, study elsewhere;
if we change our needs, you
aren't needed. Gas, like dots
of plague hidden in a rat's fur, loses
toxicity. We lie

down gasping, and the huge
host kingdom, of love's long-legged women,
and their men, stare
at our death-dancing – sharp breath,
and the slump of one mingling
in another's – the genders
are bare and swollen. In their health,
their nectared pleasing disposition,
in their long, spiritual laughter,
they stare at us.

For Vincent and Hiroko Sherry

Light needs certain gasses and the dust in the atmosphere before we may see by it

In space, space and light is passed
through dark, but in an atmosphere of dust
and breathable gasses, earth's mild
ball of space diffuses light. The bird
tramples the air.

As I look back, the island drops through
light and changes to slate, as if air were sucked from
the daytime, leaving space dark.
Before us, with the ship rocking as if
pleasured, light hazes as we come on
to the headland, its jut; in hoops
of mist stooping hills, their laps
and shelfs made as the land sat down. Underneath
the earth in discs moves
and cracks, the sea
so blue it smells of blue, open deep spaces
of it, where by the shore small fish
speckle like sand. Their shadow gives
them away. You saw them
and touched them, as you have touched me.

I draw apart the shutters. It is you says,
up. Between island and mainland each sound
turns back, turning upon itself like a cat
upon its tail of swishing fur. As the man
clasping a bow of stringed music turned
and in an instant of torches
she was gone. And he, forfeiting
the sacred grief of others, in
his unnoticing grief, was torn

87

in pieces by the women of a god.
And if air changes
its composition, we lose our life,
as a language alters and the poet,
that small fish in aspic, mouths a silent
verse where his failed language, words
in odd shaped pebble, spatter the earth.
And here, if the mild community rages
a torturer smiles at his labour; he struggles to
be worthy his hire, the organ
sheared, the feet first as a man tied
to a stretcher is fed into a furnace. Greece shimmers
into the air. The science of light holds us.

I see you, I touch you. Insects with
feet and stings ready help
themselves to that small captured piece of field,
a garden. A bird flirts a speckled wing.
In his shrine behind a door of glass – my Lord God,
emerge, please, from the small silver figure.
We've been born. Share me, have me,
friend, daughter, companion.

Postface

I read Frank Kermode's *The Genesis of Secrecy* in 1979 and
found there what touched off what are now 'Poems
concerning Salome and Herod' but which I at first called
'The Salome Poems'. In one place Kermode pauses to ask,
'how old is Salome?' In the poems, she is more than one
age. In the first she is, chronologically, about two
thousand years – though fixed in early middle age when
the most extreme point in her predicament as a woman,
trapped by early experience, has been reached; with
neither age to console her – if that is what it does – nor
youth for her to enjoy. In other poems she is a 'damsel'
but, as Kermode suggests, the term is dim and ambigu-
ous. In the end I felt that when Salome suffered Herod she
had barely entered puberty. She had in her her mother's
feelings and ambition, as well as her own early mental
tumescence. With this equipment she was easily the prey
of Herod, and Herod had nothing in him with which to
resist his desires. Herodias and her daughter formed a
double pressure on Herod and his authority and, together,
they exacted from him the life of John the Baptist in
miserable exchange for very little.

It stayed in my mind that Salome was the instrument of
this, but was also acted upon by the experience, altered in
such a way that she found herself, as it were, in a room
without window or door – not a blind room, but one
without exit. And that having drastically changed through
the experience, the alteration that she had undergone
permitted no further change or growth. Thus the harsh-

ness of these poems comes in a response to the pressure Salome both applies and suffers when she is still a child, physically, spiritually and morally. If there is bitterness in the poems it rises like gall from a still sense of how Salome – the damsel – is simplified by such pressure and in that state finally obtains harm for others and damage to herself.

I would not want the Salome poems to represent the nature of all the other poems here, but in one respect a number of the poems share the preoccupation of the Salome group – which is to do with transgression and its pain.

I am thinking of actions and their irreversible nature, of which war is an instance. It is not only to do with killing, but with the appetite we may acquire for it, the presence of mind working one way towards more of the same. We need no reminding, for our presentiment of these things is painful. So many have so often noted it all in these years, when the extent of human unhappiness, and misery produced by war or aggression, has made some ask if we will survive as a species if we continue as we are. I merely add to this that the timbre of these poems, and their preoccupations, are, all the same, connected with a different possibility for happiness, which isn't a sin. To re-enact in a certain way the condition of pain may imply the possibility of growth and happiness, and in doing this, in a poem, it may both contain and focus them in reciprocity. That at least is a working theory, and the containment of them in a poem is a way of transmitting their value to our needs. If as a result one may enjoy and value a poem, that is something, for such a close response may help one in turn to mediate between oneself and the world.

Index of first lines

91

Also by Jon Silkin

The Psalms with their Spoils

This is Jon Silkin's eighth collection of verse. Throughout, his poetic principles have remained the same, although his range of preoccupations has grown. Moral concern and a desire for growth are still his objectives; his moods intimate and immediate: pity, anger, and sensuousness. The poems are close-knit, Silkin continuing his exploration of the interaction between narrative and imagism, sharpening his syntax and straightening its direction.

Selected Poems

Jon Silkin's first collection of poetry, *The Peaceable Kingdom*, was published in 1954, and was described by the distinguished American critic Merle Brown as 'the finest first volume of poetry written by a living English poet.' Six further collections followed, up to the publication of *The Little Time-Keeper* in 1976. From these seven collections is drawn the selection made in this volume.